FREDERICK WARNE
Published by the Penguin Group
Penguin Books Ltd, 27 Wrights Lane, London W8 5TZ, England
Penguin Putnam Inc., 375 Hudson Street, New York, NY 10014, USA
Penguin Books Australia Ltd, Ringwood, Victoria, Australia
Penguin Books Canada Ltd, 10 Alcorn Avenue, Toronto, Ontario, Canada M4V
3B2
Penguin Books (N.Z.) Ltd, 182-190 Wairau Road, Auckland 10, New Zealand

Penguin Books Ltd, Registered Offices: Harmondsworth, Middlesex, England

First published in 1999

1 3 5 7 9 10 8 6 4 2

ISBN 07232 4537 1

Printed in China by Imago Publishing Ltd.

The Flower Fairies™

☀ Address Book ☀

FREDERICK WARNE

A

Apple Blossom

Name

Address

Telephone

Name

Address

Telephone

Name

Address

Telephone

Name

Address

Telephone

Name

Address

Telephone

Name

Address

Telephone

Name

Address

Telephone

Name

Address

Telephone

Name

Address

Telephone

Name

Address

Telephone

A

Name _____
Address _____
_____

Telephone _____

Name _____
Address _____
_____

Telephone _____

Name _____
Address _____
_____

Telephone _____

Name _____
Address _____
_____

Telephone _____

Name _____
Address _____
_____

Telephone _____

Name _____
Address _____
_____

Telephone _____

Name _____
Address _____
_____

Telephone _____

Name _____
Address _____
_____

Telephone _____

Name _____
Address _____
_____

Telephone _____

Name _____
Address _____
_____

Telephone _____

Name _____
Address _____
_____

Telephone _____

Name _____
Address _____
_____

Telephone _____

A

Name
Address

Telephone

Name
Address

Telephone

Name
Address

Telephone

Name
Address

Telephone

Name
Address

Telephone

Name
Address

Telephone

Name
Address

Telephone

Name
Address

Telephone

Name
Address

Telephone

Name
Address

Telephone

Name
Address

Telephone

Name
Address

Telephone

B

Bugle

B

Name

Address

Telephone

Name

Address

Telephone

Name

Address

Telephone

Name

Address

Telephone

Name

Address

Telephone

Name

Address

Telephone

Name

Address

Telephone

Name

Address

Telephone

B

Name

Address

Telephone

Name

Address

Telephone

Name

Address

Telephone

Name

Address

Telephone

Name

Address

Telephone

Name

Address

Telephone

Name

Address

Telephone

Name

Address

Telephone

Name

Address

Telephone

Name

Address

Telephone

Name

Address

Telephone

Name

Address

Telephone

B

Name

Address

Telephone

Name

Address

Telephone

Name

Address

Telephone

Name

Address

Telephone

Name

Address

Telephone

Name

Address

Telephone

Name

Address

Telephone

Name

Address

Telephone

Name

Address

Telephone

Name

Address

Telephone

Name

Address

Telephone

Name

Address

Telephone

Columbine

C

Name

Address

Telephone

Name

Address

Telephone

Name

Address

Telephone

Name

Address

Telephone

Name

Address

Telephone

Name

Address

Telephone

Name

Address

Telephone

Name

Address

Telephone

C

Name
Address

Telephone

Name
Address

Telephone

Name
Address

Telephone

Name
Address

Telephone

Name
Address

Telephone

Name
Address

Telephone

Name
Address

Telephone

Name
Address

Telephone

Name
Address

Telephone

Name
Address

Telephone

Name
Address

Telephone

Name
Address

Telephone

$\mathcal{C}$

Name

Address

Telephone

Name

Address

Telephone

Name

Address

Telephone

Name

Address

Telephone

Name

Address

Telephone

Name

Address

Telephone

Name

Address

Telephone

Name

Address

Telephone

Name

Address

Telephone

Name

Address

Telephone

Name

Address

Telephone

Name

Address

Telephone

D

Double Daisy

Name _____   Name _____
Address _____   Address _____
_____   _____

Telephone _____   Telephone _____

Name _____   Name _____
Address _____   Address _____
_____   _____

Telephone _____   Telephone _____

Name _____   Name _____
Address _____   Address _____
_____   _____

Telephone _____   Telephone _____

Name _____   Name _____
Address _____   Address _____
_____   _____

Telephone _____   Telephone _____

Name _____   Name _____
Address _____   Address _____
_____   _____

Telephone _____   Telephone _____

$\mathcal{D}$

Name	Name
Address	Address
Telephone	Telephone
Name	Name
Address	Address
Telephone	Telephone
Name	Name
Address	Address
Telephone	Telephone
Name	Name
Address	Address
Telephone	Telephone
Name	Name
Address	Address
Telephone	Telephone
Name	Name
Address	Address
Telephone	Telephone

D

Name
Address

Telephone

Name
Address

Telephone

Name
Address

Telephone

Name
Address

Telephone

Name
Address

Telephone

Name
Address

Telephone

Name
Address

Telephone

Name
Address

Telephone

Name
Address

Telephone

Name
Address

Telephone

Name
Address

Telephone

Name
Address

Telephone

E

Eyebright

Name	*Name*
Address	*Address*
Telephone	*Telephone*
Name	*Name*
Address	*Address*
Telephone	*Telephone*
Name	*Name*
Address	*Address*
Telephone	*Telephone*
Name	*Name*
Address	*Address*
Telephone	*Telephone*
Name	*Name*
Address	*Address*
Telephone	*Telephone*

Name

Address

Telephone

Name

Address

Telephone

Name

Address

Telephone

Name

Address

Telephone

Name

Address

Telephone

Name

Address

Telephone

Name

Address

Telephone

Name

Address

Telephone

Name

Address

Telephone

Name

Address

Telephone

Name

Address

Telephone

Name

Address

Telephone

Name

Address

Telephone

Name

Address

Telephone

Name

Address

Telephone

Name

Address

Telephone

Name

Address

Telephone

Name

Address

Telephone

Name

Address

Telephone

Name

Address

Telephone

Name

Address

Telephone

Name

Address

Telephone

Name

Address

Telephone

Name

Address

Telephone

F

Fuchsia

Name
Address

Telephone

Name
Address

Telephone

Name
Address

Telephone

Name
Address

Telephone

Name
Address

Telephone

Name
Address

Telephone

Name
Address

Telephone

Name
Address

Telephone

Name
Address

Telephone

Name
Address

Telephone

F

Name _____
Address _____
_____
Telephone _____

Name _____
Address _____
_____
Telephone _____

Name _____
Address _____
_____
Telephone _____

Name _____
Address _____
_____
Telephone _____

Name _____
Address _____
_____
Telephone _____

Name _____
Address _____
_____
Telephone _____

Name _____
Address _____
_____
Telephone _____

Name _____
Address _____
_____
Telephone _____

Name _____
Address _____
_____
Telephone _____

Name _____
Address _____
_____
Telephone _____

Name _____
Address _____
_____
Telephone _____

Name _____
Address _____
_____
Telephone _____

F

Name	*Name*
Address	*Address*
Telephone	*Telephone*
Name	*Name*
Address	*Address*
Telephone	*Telephone*
Name	*Name*
Address	*Address*
Telephone	*Telephone*
Name	*Name*
Address	*Address*
Telephone	*Telephone*
Name	*Name*
Address	*Address*
Telephone	*Telephone*
Name	*Name*
Address	*Address*
Telephone	*Telephone*

G

Gorse

G

Name
Address

Telephone

Name
Address

Telephone

Name
Address

Telephone

Name
Address

Telephone

Name
Address

Telephone

Name
Address

Telephone

Name
Address

Telephone

Name
Address

Telephone

G

Name

Address

Telephone

Name

Address

Telephone

Name

Address

Telephone

Name

Address

Telephone

Name

Address

Telephone

Name

Address

Telephone

Name

Address

Telephone

Name

Address

Telephone

Name

Address

Telephone

Name

Address

Telephone

Name

Address

Telephone

Name

Address

Telephone

G

Name	Name
Address	Address
Telephone	Telephone
Name	Name
Address	Address
Telephone	Telephone
Name	Name
Address	Address
Telephone	Telephone
Name	Name
Address	Address
Telephone	Telephone
Name	Name
Address	Address
Telephone	Telephone
Name	Name
Address	Address
Telephone	Telephone

Herb Twopence

H

Name _____
Address _____
_____
Telephone _____

Name _____
Address _____
_____
Telephone _____

Name _____
Address _____
_____
Telephone _____

Name _____
Address _____
_____
Telephone _____

Name _____
Address _____
_____
Telephone _____

Name _____
Address _____
_____
Telephone _____

Name _____
Address _____
_____
Telephone _____

Name _____
Address _____
_____
Telephone _____

Name _____
Address _____
_____
Telephone _____

Name _____
Address _____
_____
Telephone _____

$\mathcal{H}$

Name	Name
Address	Address
Telephone	Telephone
Name	Name
Address	Address
Telephone	Telephone
Name	Name
Address	Address
Telephone	Telephone
Name	Name
Address	Address
Telephone	Telephone
Name	Name
Address	Address
Telephone	Telephone
Name	Name
Address	Address
Telephone	Telephone

H

Name _____
Address _____
_____

Telephone _____

Name _____
Address _____
_____

Telephone _____

Name _____
Address _____
_____

Telephone _____

Name _____
Address _____
_____

Telephone _____

Name _____
Address _____
_____

Telephone _____

Name _____
Address _____
_____

Telephone _____

Name _____
Address _____
_____

Telephone _____

Name _____
Address _____
_____

Telephone _____

Name _____
Address _____
_____

Telephone _____

Name _____
Address _____
_____

Telephone _____

Name _____
Address _____
_____

Telephone _____

Name _____
Address _____
_____

Telephone _____

I

Iris

Name

Address

Telephone

Name

Address

Telephone

Name

Address

Telephone

Name

Address

Telephone

Name

Address

Telephone

Name

Address

Telephone

Name

Address

Telephone

Name

Address

Telephone

Name

Address

Telephone

Name

Address

Telephone

J

Name

Address

Telephone

Name

Address

Telephone

Name

Address

Telephone

Name

Address

Telephone

Name

Address

Telephone

Name

Address

Telephone

Name

Address

Telephone

Name

Address

Telephone

Name

Address

Telephone

Name

Address

Telephone

J

Name
Address

Telephone

Name
Address

Telephone

Name
Address

Telephone

Name
Address

Telephone

Name
Address

Telephone

Name
Address

Telephone

Name
Address

Telephone

Name
Address

Telephone

Name
Address

Telephone

Name
Address

Telephone

Name
Address

Telephone

Name
Address

Telephone

J

Jasmine

Name
Address

Telephone

Name
Address

Telephone

Name
Address

Telephone

Name
Address

Telephone

Name
Address

Telephone

Name
Address

Telephone

Name
Address

Telephone

Name
Address

Telephone

Name
Address

Telephone

Name
Address

Telephone

J

Name
Address

Telephone

Name
Address

Telephone

Name
Address

Telephone

Name
Address

Telephone

Name
Address

Telephone

Name
Address

Telephone

Name
Address

Telephone

Name
Address

Telephone

Name
Address

Telephone

Name
Address

Telephone

Name
Address

Telephone

Name
Address

Telephone

J

Name

Address

Telephone

Name

Address

Telephone

Name

Address

Telephone

Name

Address

Telephone

Name

Address

Telephone

Name

Address

Telephone

Name

Address

Telephone

Name

Address

Telephone

Name

Address

Telephone

Name

Address

Telephone

Name

Address

Telephone

Name

Address

Telephone

K

Kingcup

K

Name	*Name*
Address	*Address*
Telephone	*Telephone*
Name	*Name*
Address	*Address*
Telephone	*Telephone*
Name	*Name*
Address	*Address*
Telephone	*Telephone*
Name	*Name*
Address	*Address*
Telephone	*Telephone*
Name	*Name*
Address	*Address*
Telephone	*Telephone*

K

Name _____
Address _____
_____

Telephone _____

Name _____
Address _____
_____

Telephone _____

Name _____
Address _____
_____

Telephone _____

Name _____
Address _____
_____

Telephone _____

Name _____
Address _____
_____

Telephone _____

Name _____
Address _____
_____

Telephone _____

Name _____
Address _____
_____

Telephone _____

Name _____
Address _____
_____

Telephone _____

Name _____
Address _____
_____

Telephone _____

Name _____
Address _____
_____

Telephone _____

Name _____
Address _____
_____

Telephone _____

Name _____
Address _____
_____

Telephone _____

K

Name
Address

Telephone

Name
Address

Telephone

Name
Address

Telephone

Name
Address

Telephone

Name
Address

Telephone

Name
Address

Telephone

Name
Address

Telephone

Name
Address

Telephone

Name
Address

Telephone

Name
Address

Telephone

Name
Address

Telephone

Name
Address

Telephone

L

Lily-of-the-Valley

Name _____   Name _____
  Address _____   Address _____
  _____   _____

Telephone _____   Telephone _____

Name _____   Name _____
  Address _____   Address _____
  _____   _____

Telephone _____   Telephone _____

Name _____   Name _____
  Address _____   Address _____
  _____   _____

Telephone _____   Telephone _____

Name _____   Name _____
  Address _____   Address _____
  _____   _____

Telephone _____   Telephone _____

Name _____   Name _____
  Address _____   Address _____
  _____   _____

Telephone _____   Telephone _____

L

L

Name
Address

Telephone

Name
Address

Telephone

Name
Address

Telephone

Name
Address

Telephone

Name
Address

Telephone

Name
Address

Telephone

Name
Address

Telephone

Name
Address

Telephone

Name
Address

Telephone

Name
Address

Telephone

Name
Address

Telephone

Name
Address

Telephone

L

Name	Name
Address	Address
Telephone	Telephone
Name	Name
Address	Address
Telephone	Telephone
Name	Name
Address	Address
Telephone	Telephone
Name	Name
Address	Address
Telephone	Telephone
Name	Name
Address	Address
Telephone	Telephone
Name	Name
Address	Address
Telephone	Telephone

M

Mallow

M

Name	Name
Address	Address
Telephone	Telephone
Name	Name
Address	Address
Telephone	Telephone
Name	Name
Address	Address
Telephone	Telephone
Name	Name
Address	Address
Telephone	Telephone
Name	Name
Address	Address
Telephone	Telephone

M

Name _____
Address _____
_____
_____
Telephone _____

Name _____
Address _____
_____
_____
Telephone _____

Name _____
Address _____
_____
_____
Telephone _____

Name _____
Address _____
_____
_____
Telephone _____

Name _____
Address _____
_____
_____
Telephone _____

Name _____
Address _____
_____
_____
Telephone _____

Name _____
Address _____
_____
_____
Telephone _____

Name _____
Address _____
_____
_____
Telephone _____

Name _____
Address _____
_____
_____
Telephone _____

Name _____
Address _____
_____
_____
Telephone _____

Name
Address

Telephone

Name
Address

Telephone

Name
Address

Telephone

Name
Address

Telephone

Name
Address

Telephone

Name
Address

Telephone

Name
Address

Telephone

Name
Address

Telephone

Name
Address

Telephone

Name
Address

Telephone

Name
Address

Telephone

Name
Address

Telephone

N

Nasturtium

Name	Name
Address	Address
Telephone	Telephone
Name	Name
Address	Address
Telephone	Telephone
Name	Name
Address	Address
Telephone	Telephone
Name	Name
Address	Address
Telephone	Telephone
Name	Name
Address	Address
Telephone	Telephone

N

Name

Address

Telephone

Name

Address

Telephone

Name

Address

Telephone

Name

Address

Telephone

Name

Address

Telephone

Name

Address

Telephone

Name

Address

Telephone

Name

Address

Telephone

Name

Address

Telephone

Name

Address

Telephone

Name

Address

Telephone

Name

Address

Telephone

N

Name

Address

Telephone

Name

Address

Telephone

Name

Address

Telephone

Name

Address

Telephone

Name

Address

Telephone

Name

Address

Telephone

Name

Address

Telephone

Name

Address

Telephone

Name

Address

Telephone

Name

Address

Telephone

Name

Address

Telephone

Name

Address

Telephone

Orchis

Name

Address

Telephone

Name

Address

Telephone

Name

Address

Telephone

Name

Address

Telephone

Name

Address

Telephone

Name

Address

Telephone

Name

Address

Telephone

Name

Address

Telephone

Name

Address

Telephone

Name

Address

Telephone

O

 O

Name
Address

Telephone

Name
Address

Telephone

Name
Address

Telephone

Name
Address

Telephone

Name
Address

Telephone

Name
Address

Telephone

Name
Address

Telephone

Name
Address

Telephone

Name
Address

Telephone

Name
Address

Telephone

O

Name

Address

Telephone

Name

Address

Telephone

Name

Address

Telephone

Name

Address

Telephone

Name

Address

Telephone

Name

Address

Telephone

Name

Address

Telephone

Name

Address

Telephone

Name

Address

Telephone

Name

Address

Telephone

Name

Address

Telephone

Name

Address

Telephone

P

Pansy

P Q

Name _____
Address _____
_____
Telephone _____

Name _____
Address _____
_____
Telephone _____

Name _____
Address _____
_____
Telephone _____

Name _____
Address _____
_____
Telephone _____

Name _____
Address _____
_____
Telephone _____

Name _____
Address _____
_____
Telephone _____

Name _____
Address _____
_____
Telephone _____

Name _____
Address _____
_____
Telephone _____

Name _____
Address _____
_____
Telephone _____

Name _____
Address _____
_____
Telephone _____

P Q

Name

Address

Telephone

Name

Address

Telephone

Name

Address

Telephone

Name

Address

Telephone

Name

Address

Telephone

Name

Address

Telephone

Name

Address

Telephone

Name

Address

Telephone

Name

Address

Telephone

Name

Address

Telephone

Name

Address

Telephone

Name

Address

Telephone

P2

Name	Name
Address	Address
Telephone	Telephone
Name	Name
Address	Address
Telephone	Telephone
Name	Name
Address	Address
Telephone	Telephone
Name	Name
Address	Address
Telephone	Telephone
Name	Name
Address	Address
Telephone	Telephone
Name	Name
Address	Address
Telephone	Telephone

R

Ragged Robin

R

Name

Address

Telephone

Name

Address

Telephone

Name

Address

Telephone

Name

Address

Telephone

Name

Address

Telephone

Name

Address

Telephone

Name

Address

Telephone

Name

Address

Telephone

Name

Address

Telephone

Name

Address

Telephone

R

R

Name _____

Address _____

_____

Telephone _____

Name _____

Address _____

_____

Telephone _____

Name _____

Address _____

_____

Telephone _____

Name _____

Address _____

_____

Telephone _____

Name _____

Address _____

_____

Telephone _____

Name _____

Address _____

_____

Telephone _____

Name _____

Address _____

_____

Telephone _____

Name _____

Address _____

_____

Telephone _____

Name _____

Address _____

_____

Telephone _____

Name _____

Address _____

_____

Telephone _____

Name _____

Address _____

_____

Telephone _____

Name _____

Address _____

_____

Telephone _____

R

Name

Address

Telephone

Name

Address

Telephone

Name

Address

Telephone

Name

Address

Telephone

Name

Address

Telephone

Name

Address

Telephone

Name

Address

Telephone

Name

Address

Telephone

Name

Address

Telephone

Name

Address

Telephone

Name

Address

Telephone

Name

Address

Telephone

S

Strawberry

Name

Address

Telephone

Name

Address

Telephone

Name

Address

Telephone

Name

Address

Telephone

Name

Address

Telephone

Name

Address

Telephone

Name

Address

Telephone

Name

Address

Telephone

Name

Address

Telephone

Name

Address

Telephone

S

S

Name

Address

Telephone

Name

Address

Telephone

Name

Address

Telephone

Name

Address

Telephone

Name

Address

Telephone

Name

Address

Telephone

Name

Address

Telephone

Name

Address

Telephone

Name

Address

Telephone

Name

Address

Telephone

Name

Address

Telephone

Name

Address

Telephone

S

Name
Address

Telephone

Name
Address

Telephone

Name
Address

Telephone

Name
Address

Telephone

Name
Address

Telephone

Name
Address

Telephone

Name
Address

Telephone

Name
Address

Telephone

Name
Address

Telephone

Name
Address

Telephone

Name
Address

Telephone

Name
Address

Telephone

T

Thrift

Name
Address

Telephone

Name
Address

Telephone

Name
Address

Telephone

Name
Address

Telephone

Name
Address

Telephone

Name
Address

Telephone

Name
Address

Telephone

Name
Address

Telephone

Name
Address

Telephone

Name
Address

Telephone

T

T

Name

Address

Telephone

Name

Address

Telephone

Name

Address

Telephone

Name

Address

Telephone

Name

Address

Telephone

Name

Address

Telephone

Name

Address

Telephone

Name

Address

Telephone

Name

Address

Telephone

Name

Address

Telephone

Name

Address

Telephone

Name

Address

Telephone

T

Name	Name
Address	Address
Telephone	Telephone
Name	Name
Address	Address
Telephone	Telephone
Name	Name
Address	Address
Telephone	Telephone
Name	Name
Address	Address
Telephone	Telephone
Name	Name
Address	Address
Telephone	Telephone
Name	Name
Address	Address
Telephone	Telephone

UV

Vetch

UV

Name
Address

Telephone

Name
Address

Telephone

Name
Address

Telephone

Name
Address

Telephone

Name
Address

Telephone

Name
Address

Telephone

Name
Address

Telephone

Name
Address

Telephone

Name
Address

Telephone

Name
Address

Telephone

U V

Name
Address

Telephone

Name
Address

Telephone

Name
Address

Telephone

Name
Address

Telephone

Name
Address

Telephone

Name
Address

Telephone

Name
Address

Telephone

Name
Address

Telephone

Name
Address

Telephone

Name
Address

Telephone

Name
Address

Telephone

Name
Address

Telephone

U V

Name

Address

Telephone

Name

Address

Telephone

Name

Address

Telephone

Name

Address

Telephone

Name

Address

Telephone

Name

Address

Telephone

Name

Address

Telephone

Name

Address

Telephone

Name

Address

Telephone

Name

Address

Telephone

Name

Address

Telephone

Name

Address

Telephone

Wallflower

Name	Name
Address	Address
Telephone	Telephone
Name	Name
Address	Address
Telephone	Telephone
Name	Name
Address	Address
Telephone	Telephone
Name	Name
Address	Address
Telephone	Telephone
Name	Name
Address	Address
Telephone	Telephone

W

$\mathcal{W}$

Name _____
Address _____
_____
Telephone _____

Name _____
Address _____
_____
Telephone _____

Name _____
Address _____
_____
Telephone _____

Name _____
Address _____
_____
Telephone _____

Name _____
Address _____
_____
Telephone _____

Name _____
Address _____
_____
Telephone _____

Name _____
Address _____
_____
Telephone _____

Name _____
Address _____
_____
Telephone _____

Name _____
Address _____
_____
Telephone _____

Name _____
Address _____
_____
Telephone _____

Name

Address

Telephone

Name

Address

Telephone

Name

Address

Telephone

Name

Address

Telephone

Name

Address

Telephone

Name

Address

Telephone

Name

Address

Telephone

Name

Address

Telephone

Name

Address

Telephone

Name

Address

Telephone

XY

Yellow Deadnettle

X Y Z

Name	Name
Address	Address
Telephone	Telephone
Name	Name
Address	Address
Telephone	Telephone
Name	Name
Address	Address
Telephone	Telephone
Name	Name
Address	Address
Telephone	Telephone
Name	Name
Address	Address
Telephone	Telephone

X Y Z

Name	Name
Address	Address
Telephone	Telephone
Name	Name
Address	Address
Telephone	Telephone
Name	Name
Address	Address
Telephone	Telephone
Name	Name
Address	Address
Telephone	Telephone
Name	Name
Address	Address
Telephone	Telephone
Name	Name
Address	Address
Telephone	Telephone

XYZ

Name
Address

Telephone

Name
Address

Telephone

Name
Address

Telephone

Name
Address

Telephone

Name
Address

Telephone

Name
Address

Telephone

Name
Address

Telephone

Name
Address

Telephone

Name
Address

Telephone

Name
Address

Telephone

Name
Address

Telephone

Name
Address

Telephone